BEES AND WASPS

Anne Smith

Wayland

Nature Study

Bees and Wasps
Frogs and Toads
Rabbits and Hares
Snakes and Lizards
Spiders
Worms

Cover: An Australian flower wasp.

Frontispiece: A honey-bee gathers pollen from a flower.

This book is based on an original text by Christopher O'Toole.

First published in 1989 by
Wayland (Publishers) Ltd
61 Western Road, Hove
East Sussex BN3 1JD, England

© Copyright 1989 Wayland (Publishers) Ltd

Edited by Alison Cooper

British Library Cataloguing in Publication Data
Smith, Anne
   Bees and Wasps
   1. Bees and Wasps
   I. Title   II. Series

ISBN 1–85210–771–5

Typeset by Kalligraphics Ltd, Horley, Surrey
Printed in Italy by G. Canale and C.S.p.A., Turin
Bound in France by A.G.M.

Contents

Words written in
bold are explained
in the glossary.

Introducing bees and wasps

The bee and wasp family

There are thousands of different kinds of bee and wasp.

This common wasp is drinking **nectar** from an ivy flower.

Bees and wasps live in every country of the world. The common black and yellow wasps live together in a **colony**. So do honey-bees and furry bumblebees. They are called **social** insects. Almost all the other kinds of bee and wasp live alone. They are called **solitary** insects. Some of them make nests.

This is a sawfly. It does not make a nest. The female has a special egg-laying tube. She uses it to make a slit in a leaf or stem. Then she lays an egg in the slit. The sawfly grubs eat leaves.

Bees and wasps in close-up

The skeleton of a bee or wasp is on the outside of its body. It covers the three main parts of the body: the head, **thorax** and **abdomen**.

Female bees and wasps have a sting like this at the tip of the abdomen. They use it to poison their enemies.

Bees and wasps have two pairs of wings. They have six legs, like all insects. This honey-bee has **pollen** baskets on its legs.

All wasps that make nests feed their grubs on small insects. Bees feed their young on pollen and nectar from flowers.

Bees are covered with hairs like fur. Pollen collects on the hairs as the bees go in and out of the flowers. The bees scrape the pollen off into special pollen baskets on their back legs.

The body of a honey-bee

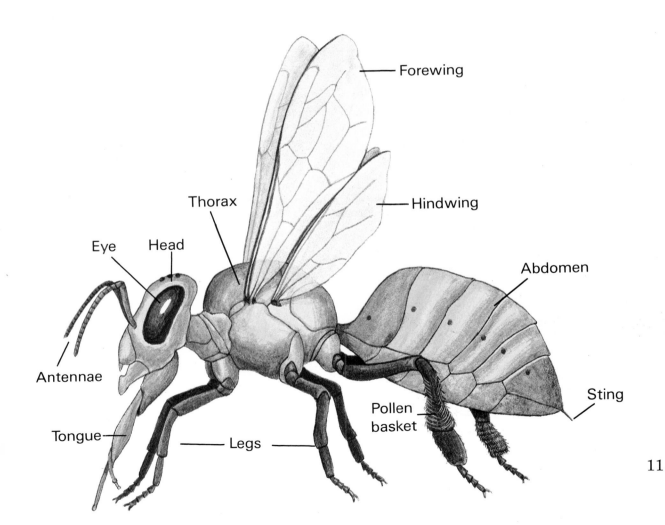

11

The nest

Most bees and wasps make nests. They lay their eggs and store food in them.

◀ These sand bees nest in burrows in the soil. There are many other kinds of nest. Some bees and wasps use holes in wood which have been made by other insects.

◀ Common wasps make nests out of tiny pieces of chewed wood.

The mud-dauber wasp makes her nest out of damp mud.

When the female bee or wasp has built her nest, she flies all round the entrance. She looks at landmarks like trees, rocks and hills. She looks at where the sun is in the sky. All these things will help her to find her way home.

Finding a mate

Male bees and wasps do not help the females to make nests or find food. When they are ready to mate, some males fly around the flowers looking for females. Male solitary bees mate many times. Females usually mate only once.

Some male wasps wait for the females to come out of the nest.

➡

Male cotton-wool bees have a special place where they wait among the flowers. This is their territory. They mate with any female who comes there.

Male bumblebees leave a special scent on leaves. It attracts females who have not mated.

Solitary bees and wasps

Skinny hunting wasps

The skinny hunting wasp is a solitary insect. It is called the skinny hunting wasp because it is long and thin. This wasp lives alone but many thousands can live near each other in the same patch of earth.

The females make their ▶ nests in the sand. They spend the night hanging on to a grass stem with their jaws.

The female makes a short tunnel. Then she makes a **cell** in the nest to store food. This wasp has filled her nest with food. She is closing the entrance to the nest with a lump of soil.

➡

⬆

When the sun comes up, the wasps start to fly. The males mate with the females. When a female has mated, she digs out a nest.

Next morning, the skinny hunting wasp flies off. She hunts for caterpillars among the leaves. When she finds one, she takes it to her nest cell. She lays an egg on the caterpillar. Then she closes up the nest with a pebble. She needs energy, so she visits flowers to eat nectar. Then she can go on hunting for caterpillars.

This wasp nest is full of caterpillars. One has an egg on it. ▶

These females are trying to steal a caterpillar from another female.

▼

When the wasp grub hatches, it eats the caterpillars. Then it spins a **cocoon** around itself. By the next summer, it will have become an adult wasp.

Mining bees

There are thousands of different kinds of mining bee. They come out in very early spring.

This sand bee is a mining bee. It has a striped abdomen. In the summer it nests in old sand-pits or in sandy places near the sea.

This is a tawny mining bee. The female has a coat of red hairs. The male has a coat of brown hairs.

Mining bees make cells at the end of tunnels in the ground. They fill the cells with pollen and nectar. Then they lay one egg in each cell. When the young bees hatch they feed on the pollen and the nectar.

Mason bees

Mason bees make nests in ready-made holes. These can be in dead wood or walls. The female makes a row of nesting cells. She fills each cell with pollen and nectar for food. She lays one egg in each cell. This mason bee is closing the cell with mud.

This is a mason-bee grub. It eats the yellow pollen and nectar. Then it spins a cocoon around itself. It stays in the cell until it has grown and the weather is warmer. It bites its way out of the cocoon in the spring.

Leafcutter bees and cotton-wool bees

Leafcutter bees make nests in ready-made holes too. They cut pieces of leaf to line the nest tunnel. They stick the pieces together with **sap**.

This is the nest of a leafcutter bee. Each cell has a young grub inside it. The grubs are feeding on a store of pollen and nectar.

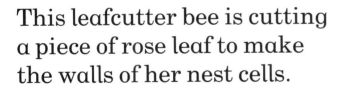

This leafcutter bee is cutting a piece of rose leaf to make the walls of her nest cells.

This is a cotton-wool bee. It lines its nest with soft hairs. It is collecting hairs from a lamb's ears plant.

Parasites and galls

These wasp grubs are living ▶ inside a gall. They do not have a nest.

Some wasps lay their eggs in a leaf-bud or stem. Then the plant grows round the eggs. This makes a kind of ball that is called a gall. The grubs live inside the gall and eat it.

◀ This is a gall on a rose bush.

This caterpillar is being eaten by wasp grubs. Wasps that lay their eggs in the bodies of other insects are called parasites. The **host** insects are still alive. When the grubs hatch, they eat the host insects and kill them. Some parasites are useful to people because they feed on caterpillars that eat the cabbage crops.

This parasite wasp can bore through wood to lay eggs on other insects.

27

Social bees and wasps

Living together

These are paper wasps. They have made a nest that feels like paper. Paper wasps live in warm parts of the world. They are social insects. Social bees and wasps live together in family groups. Each group is called a colony.

A colony has one female who lays the eggs. She is called the queen. There are hundreds of female workers who do not lay eggs. The workers collect food and feed the young every day.

This paper wasp is collecting nectar from a flower.

When the male wasps in the colony hatch, they mate with the females. The young queens fly off to build new nests.

Social wasps and hornets

The black and yellow wasps found in colder countries are sometimes called yellow jackets. They like jam and rotting fruit.

This hornet is a big yellow jacket. It makes nests in hollow trees.

This queen wasp has made a nest outside a house.

The queen yellow jacket hibernates over the winter. In the spring, she makes a nest from a kind of paper. When the female wasps hatch, they become the workers. A colony can have 15,000 workers.

This is the inside of the wasp's nest. Each layer contains many cells. At the end of the summer, all the wasps in the nest die, except for the young queens. They hibernate until the following spring.

Bumblebees

The queen bumblebee makes a nest in a clump of grass. She makes a small pot using wax from her body. She fills it with eggs, pollen and honey. This is a brood cell.

This bumblebee queen is sitting on the brood cell to keep the grubs warm.

When the workers hatch, they make more brood cells for the queen. The queen goes on laying eggs. The new queens **hibernate** in winter but the rest of the colony is killed by the first frost.

These workers have just hatched.

Bumblebees like this one live in northern countries. You can see them among the spring and summer flowers.

Honey-bees – how the colony works

Beekeepers keep bees in special wooden nests called hives. There is one queen bee in each colony. She is the one marked by the yellow dot in the picture. She can lay more than 1,000 eggs a day.

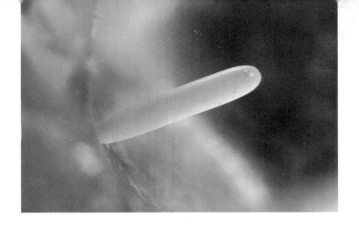

This is a honey-bee's egg in its cell. Each cell has six sides and they all fit together into a big wax **comb**.

When the old queen starts to lay fewer eggs, she leaves the hive with some workers. This is called a swarm. A young queen takes the old queen's place. She mates with the male bees. Male bees are called drones.

When they hatch, all the grubs are fed on royal jelly for three days by the workers. Royal jelly comes from **glands** in the workers' heads. After three days, worker grubs are fed on pollen and honey. Only the queen grubs are still fed on royal jelly.

These honey-bee grubs are fully grown.

A worker's life

The worker honey-bee has many jobs. She cleans the nest and looks after the young. She builds new cells and collects pollen and nectar from bees who bring it back to the nest. When she is older, she guards the nest entrance. She stings any enemies who try to come near. She spends the rest of her life collecting pollen and nectar in the fields. She tells other bees where to find the best food by two special kinds of dance.

The Round Dance

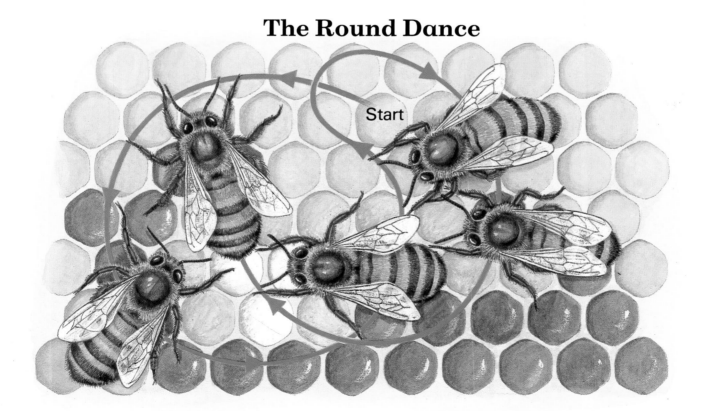

If she dances in circles, they know that the best food is near to the nest. This is called the round dance. If she dances from side to side, they know that the best food is further away. This is called the waggle dance.

This worker bee is drinking from a pond.

The Waggle Dance

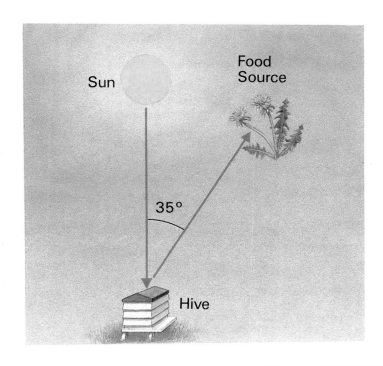

The enemies of bees and wasps

Cuckoo bees and wasps

Cuckoo bees and wasps are cheats. They lay their eggs in the nests of other bees and wasps. When the mother bee or wasp leaves to collect food, the cuckoo bee or wasp pops in and lays her egg. The cuckoo's egg hatches quickly. It eats the other egg or grub and any stored food.

This female cuckoo wasp is looking for a nest.

This female cuckoo bee has no pollen basket because she does not have to feed her young herself. Cuckoo bumblebees lay their eggs in the nests of other bumblebees. They know that the worker bees will feed their young.

Other enemies

Bees and wasps have many enemies. A large honey-bee nest is full of grubs and has a good store of honey. Chimpanzees, orang-utans and even toads and yellow-jacket wasps steal from honey-bee nests.

This bird is the African bee-eater. It knocks the bees against a branch to destroy their stings. Then it eats them.

The ratel, or African honey badger, eats bees too. It is often led to the nest by a bird called a honey guide. This bird eats beeswax. The ratel follows the bird to the nest. It breaks open the nest and eats the bees.

Bees, flowers and people

Flowers and bees are partners

Bees carry pollen from flower to flower. Pollen is made from the male parts of flowers. It needs to be mixed with the eggs made by the female parts of flowers. Bees mix the pollen and eggs. This is called pollination. Flowers make sweet nectar. Bees collect the nectar to make honey. They take the pollen for food too.

This bee collects pollen from sunflowers.

This orchid bee is visiting a tropical flower.

Bees and people

Leafcutter bees live in this special shed. They pollinate the crops that farmers need to feed their cattle. Beehives in an orchard help fruit farmers too. The bees pollinate the blossom on the fruit trees. People have kept bees for honey for thousands of years. Bees help people in lots of ways.

Mason bees and leafcutter bees will nest in drinking straws packed in a tin can. If you make a bee house like any of these you can hang it in a sunny place and watch the bees going in and out.

Bees only sting if they are roughly handled but beekeepers often wear protective clothing like this – just in case!

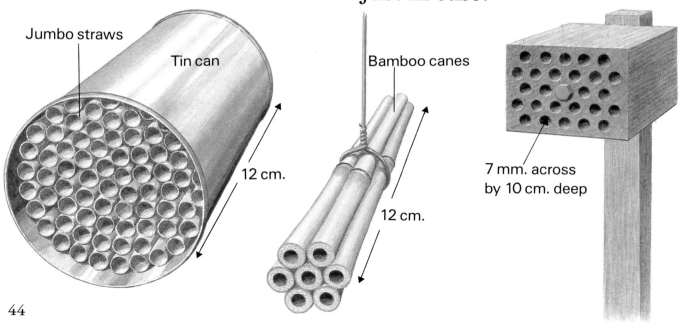

Jumbo straws

Tin can

12 cm.

Bamboo canes

12 cm.

7 mm. across by 10 cm. deep

Glossary

Abdomen   The third part of an insect's body. It contains the stomach, wax glands, sting and poison glands.

Cell   A special place in the bee's nest, where food is stored, eggs are laid and where the young bee or wasp grows.

Cocoon   The silky case which many insect grubs spin around themselves.

Colony   The nest or family where social insects live.

Comb   Rows of six-sided cells in a beehive. The bees make them from wax.

Glands   Special parts of the body which make scents or wax.

Hibernates   Sleeps through the winter.

Host   An animal, insect or plant that a parasite feeds on. The parasite often kills the host.

Nectar   The sweet mix of sugars which bees collect from flowers.

Pollen   The dusty powder made by male parts of flowers.

Sap   The juice that a plant produces.

Social   Living together in a colony.

Solitary   Living alone.

Thorax   The second or middle part of an insect's body. It contains two pairs of wings and the insect's six legs.

Finding Out More

If you would like to find out more about bees and wasps, you could read the following books:

Howard E. Evans and Mary Jane West Eberhard, *The Wasps* (David and Charles, 1970)
C. G. Butler, *The World of the Honeybee* (Collins New Naturalist, 1954)
J. B. Free, *Bees and Mankind* (George Allen and Unwin, 1982)
J. B. Free and C. G. Butler, *Bumblebees* (Collins New Naturalist, 1959)
C. O'Toole and A. Raw, *A Murmur of Bees* (Oxford University Press, 1986)
Oxford Scientific Films, *Bees and Honey* (André Deutsch, 1976)
D. V. Alford, *The Life of the Bumblebee* (Davis-Poynter, 1978)
John Reynolds, *Bees and Wasps* (Wayland, 1980)

Picture Acknowledgements

Prema Photos (R. A. Preston-Mafam) 21. All other photographs from Oxford Scientific Films by the following photographers: A. Bannister 41; G. I. Bernard 8, 22, 37, 38, 39, 44; D. Clyne cover; J. A. L. Cooke, 9, 10 (top), 12 (bottom), 13, 27, 28, 30 (bottom), 42 (right); S. Dalton frontispiece; T. Owen Edmunds 40; S. Morris 14, 16, 17, 19, 29; P. O'Toole 20; A. Ramage 15, 25 (right); D. M. Shale 32, 33; P. K. Sharpe 31; T. Shepherd 23, 24, 25 (left); D. Thompson 10 (bottom), 12 (top), 18, 26 (bottom), 34, 35, 42 (left), 43; G. Thurston 30 (top); P. & W. Ward 26 (top). Artwork by Wendy Meadway.

Index

THE LIBRARY STRANMILLIS COLLEGE
This item must be returned or renewed
by the last date shown below.

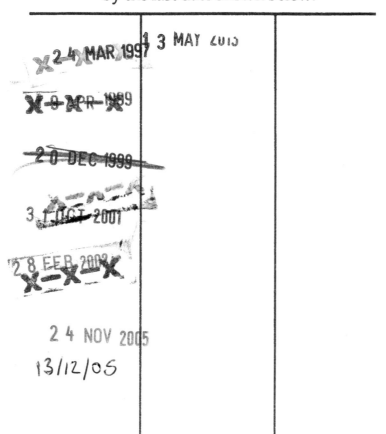